Joe went to speedway.

Joe liked speedway.

His dad was a speedway rider.

Joe's dad was in a race.

He was in front.
"Come on!" shouted Joe.

Joe's dad fell off.
"Oh no!" said Joe.

JOE

Joe's dad pushed his bike.

"What a rider!" said Joe.

It was Joe's birthday. His dad gave him a bike.

Joe liked the bike.

Joe was in a race.

He was in front.
"Come on!" shouted Dad.

Joe fell off.

"Oh no!" said Dad.

"What a rider!" said Dad.